# You Can Make a Difference

## Characteristics and Skills of the Effective Prevention Teacher

### A Guide for Educators and Other Professionals

By Linda Christensen, Ph.D.

JOHNSON INSTITUTE®

## You Can Make a Difference
**Characteristics and Skills of the Effective Prevention Teacher**

Johnson Institute
7205 Ohms Lane
Minneapolis, MN 55439-2159
(612) 831-1630

ISBN: 1-56246-028-5

Printed in the United States of America.

# Contents

**66** *I think a good teacher is one who has mastery over his or her subject, keeps up with changes in that field, remains responsive to the ever-changing needs of students, and performs a myriad of administrative tasks. Adding alcohol and other drug prevention to my teaching load concerns me. How can I gain mastery over that area and teach prevention concepts effectively in addition to everything else I'm doing? Becoming a proactive prevention resource for my students is a great idea, but I'm not sure I have what it takes to do that successfully.* **99**

# Introduction

Increasing national attention on chemical use and abuse by our young people has led educators into the role of prevention specialist. Teachers who have gained mastery over their subject areas and who have learned to become skilled teachers are now being asked to create opportunities to effectively promote alcohol and other drug use prevention in their classrooms. Teachers who begin to assume this role wonder what characteristics, skills, expertise, and approaches are needed to become effective prevention teachers.

Though the problem seems difficult, solutions abound. Teachers can take positive steps to become very good teachers of prevention. Learning the facts is, of course, a good first step. But research is telling us that the human side—our ability to listen, empathize, be available, and care—is most important in getting kids to hear, understand, and incorporate the message that use of alcohol and other drugs* is not only dangerous, but also is very "uncool."

What are the characteristics and skills that make a good prevention teacher? To uncover them, we look to what researchers have defined as the three most important areas of competency for teaching prevention:

- Teacher-student relationships
- Teacher role-modeling
- Clear information

---

* You'll notice that we use the term "alcohol and other drug(s)" throughout this booklet. We do so to emphasize that alcohol is a drug—just like cocaine, marijuana, amphetamines, depressants, or any other mood-altering chemical. Too often we hear people talk about alcohol *or* drugs or alcohol *and* drugs as if alcohol were somehow different from drugs and belonged to a category all by itself. True, our culture, our government, even our laws treat alcohol differently from the way they treat other drugs such as pot, crack, or heroin. But the symptoms of addiction are basically the same for all of these mood-altering chemicals, and the need to find ways to prevent their use is just as urgent. When we use the term "chemical dependence," it covers addiction to all of these mood-altering chemicals.

These findings indicate that leading the list is teacher-student relationships, followed closely by the teacher's ability to project an image of warmth and accessibility, and finally, strong communication skills. The teacher as source of support and referral, as a strong role model, and as a purveyor of reliable, timely, and age-appropriate information about chemical use, abuse, and consequences are also key competencies.

Teachers who have cultivated student relationships are the first to sense changes in student behavior, identify potential problems, and make suggestions for seeking help. Though the teacher's prevention role may be ambiguous, concerned teachers can increase their familiarity with resources available to guide students toward making healthy lifestyle choices.

This book will help you understand the characteristics and skills needed to become an effective prevention teacher and resource. Many of the skills and human traits that you've already cultivated in your years of teaching experience may contribute a great deal to your journey toward becoming an effective prevention teacher.

Our children face many difficult problems and decisions about alcohol or other drug use, as well as other high-risk behaviors. That's the bad news. The good news is that we, as teaching professionals, can equip ourselves to help solve these problems. Together with parents, schools, and communities, we can make a stand and work to preserve the health and well-being of our children. Together, we can make a difference.

**\*char•ac•ter•is•tic (kar'ek ter is'tik)—a distinguishing trait or quality that issues from within.**

❝ *I entered my first year of high school teaching at the ripe old age of 21, a starry-eyed idealist. All of my students were going to know grammar, literature, and come to appreciate poetry. I was going to give them my love of books and my love of learning. I was going to make a difference. Then, on graduation night, one of my students died after getting drunk and driving his car off a bridge into the Mississippi River. My grammar and poetry lessons did not keep him alive. A prevention program might have.* ❞

# Characteristics of the Effective Prevention Teacher

In the ten years I've spent training teachers in prevention work, I've often been asked why prevention is necessary. Isn't it enough, teachers ask me, that we have to teach reading, writing, arithmetic, and all the rest? The answer, unfortunately, is no. It's not enough.

Children are exposed to more high-risk behaviors now than ever before. The choices they make can result in delaying their ability to grow socially, emotionally, spiritually, and intellectually. In fact, a study by Hochhauser et al., published in the *Journal of Alcohol and Drug Education*, tells us that alcohol and other drug use can affect cognitive abilities of students in several ways: information learned is not remembered when under the influence of alcohol and drugs; alcohol or other drug use causes direct interference with the brain's ability to process information; and students are unable to concentrate while under the influence in the classroom. What good will come of teaching children to read and do long division if they don't live long enough to use those skills in the adult world?

Research by Aubrey et al. suggests that "teaching" prevention is difficult, because prevention isn't solely a cognitive-intellectual function. Instead, values and personal decision-making or affective-emotional functions are also involved.

According to Aubrey et al., this presents the teacher with several problems. First, if a teacher approaches the task of prevention as a purely cognitive one, he or she will rely heavily on presenting straight, factual information. The teacher will quickly lose ground by being unable to answer all of the students' questions, simply because alcohol and other drug education represents too large an area to cover. Secondly, discussions about prevention inevitably lead to value-laden topics. Teachers have no control or ability to enforce sanctions on behavior that takes place outside the classroom. Further, discussion of values often leads into areas where right and wrong become ambiguous. Fourth, the authoritative position of the teacher may actually block helpful, honest questioning and discussion. And finally, high-risk children's choice to use alcohol or other drugs is almost always an emotionally charged decision.

These problems can be resolved by altering the purely cognitive-intellectual approach to teaching. When we allow room for the affective-emotional aspects of a subject to emerge, we can teach more effectively. This is especially true in the case of effective prevention instruction.

Recognizing the characteristics and developing the critical skills that improve our relationship with students, our grasp of accurate information about alcohol and other drugs, and our visibility as healthy role models will not only make us more effective as prevention teachers, but more effective teachers, period. More than that, it will make each teaching day more rewarding. We'll see our students grow in their ability to process feelings, to make decisions, and to set and attain goals. We'll notice a classroom atmosphere marked by more respect and mutual trust. We'll find children becoming advocates for their own health. And we'll find ourselves enjoying our jobs more.

## Motivated

Educators enter the teaching profession for several reasons. We care deeply about children and wish to be a force for good in their lives. Or, we love a particular subject and enjoy sharing that subject with our students. Or, we want to emulate a particularly powerful teacher who influenced us in our own growing up years. Our motivation to teach comes down to a desire to share ourselves and what we know in a meaningful way with our students.

This same desire can make a good teacher of math or art or literature into an effective prevention teacher. Motivated teachers who believe in their own skills and in the value of the young minds and lives of their students can be powerful influences to help kids make better choices. Caring and believing that we can make a difference, and learning the necessary skills to do both better, will give us the warmth and interest necessary to communicate prevention principles effectively.

# Patient

Prevention isn't an event: it's a process. Mathematics isn't taught in one week in grade four. Rather, children begin to learn about numbers and mathematical functions from kindergarten through high school. In the same way, prevention is taught and demonstrated slowly, over the course of each school year. Throughout the course of a student's education, prevention concepts are introduced, taught, and reinforced in developmentally appropriate ways.

Teachers who have the benefit of a prevention curriculum in the school will find that students are exposed to information and practice in a systematic way. Skills and information provided each year build upon the previous year's curriculum, in order to reinforce prevention education in a consistent manner.

The role we play in our classroom, with or without a formal prevention curriculum, is that of a friend, resource provider, and role model. Cultivating student relationships, gaining prevention skills, and seeing students through difficult times requires patience with our students and with ourselves. Problems we encounter with a student at one age may not be resolved until a grade or two later. Likewise, problems a student experiences at one age may not be relevant at another age. The impact we have on a student may be immediate, delayed, or negligible. Patience is essential for long-term prevention effectiveness.

Remember, too, to be patient with yourself. Try to be reasonable in your expectations. Expect and strive for progress, not perfection. Allow room for mistakes. Don't beat yourself up for making mistakes. Instead, allow room for mistakes and see them as opportunities for growth.

# Bonds with Students

Each of us wants to belong, to be part of, to be linked, to be bonded with. As human beings, we feel in our bones that to *be* is to belong. Children begin their striving to belong at birth as they work to *bond* with their parents. Bonding is a process of mutual connecting on a deep emotional and spiritual level. We know that children who don't

11

bond meaningfully with others demonstrate impaired development in all areas of their lives: social, emotional, cognitive, physical and spiritual. Thus, bonding is crucial to the development of a well-adjusted child—and to the well-adjusted adult.

Bonding is especially important for effective prevention. Studies continue to confirm that children who don't feel bonded to their families, teachers, or peers are more likely to use alcohol and other drugs. These children seem unable to get fulfillment from their life experiences or from their relationships. They can be apathetic or hostile, hopeless, angry, and lonely. They find in the use of alcohol or other drugs the momentary enjoyable feelings that are missing in the rest of their lives.

These are truly high-risk children. No matter how well they master prevention concepts, they will remain significantly at risk for alcohol and other drug use unless meaningful bonds are cultivated with teachers and other students.

A study published in the *Journal of Drug Education* (Jones et al.) found that the teacher-student relationship is the most important aspect of effective prevention programs. Hospitable and welcoming teachers can make a great impact on the problem of alcohol and other drug use by establishing quality relationships with their students (Jones et al.).

According to the Jones et al. study, the top four characteristics important in a quality relationship between the student and teacher are: (1) a genuine and attentive interest in the student; (2) mutual respect; (3) honesty; and (4) good rapport. Other characteristics such as openness, developing and maintaining trust, and caring are also important.

There are many benefits to teacher-student bonding. Teachers who are open and who have bonded with students are better able to detect potential problems in their students and make appropriate referrals for help. These teachers are also more accepting of individual differences and better able to understand the motivations that underlie student behavior (Jones et al.).

Besides student-teacher bonding, hospitable teachers also encourage bonding between students. Strong peer bonds provide an important sense of connection to others and give students the added benefit of depending on each other to resist high-risk behavior.

Unhealthy peer relationships can create problems for kids. Most students who use alcohol or other drugs are introduced to them by their friends. Also, false bonds can form between students who use alcohol or other drugs together. Only real bonds, formed out of mutual respect and trust, will nurture healthy choices among peers. Thus, student-to-student bonding can be a major line of defense against use of alcohol and other drugs. Once bonding has been established, the effective prevention teacher can go on to teach students how to help each other in difficult situations, to watch out for each other, to help keep each other safe, and to respect each other's right to say no.

Any situation can be improved by adding love, compassion, empathy, and understanding. Bonding between the teacher and student and between students themselves provides the basis for teaching valuable prevention concepts in the classroom.

# Positive Role Model

The teacher who is a positive role model for his or her students makes an effective prevention teacher. Students emulate teachers who are positive role models and want to be like them. Look at this true story:

Every day when Jennifer came home from Mrs. Horton's first grade class, she played school. She set up her dolls and stuffed animals and taught them everything she had learned that day at school. When Jennifer's parents asked her what she wanted for Christmas, Jennifer told them that she wanted all the "stuff" that Mrs. Horton had. So, Jennifer's parents bought her a small bulletin board, a lesson plan book, a grade book, workbooks, construction paper, markers, and crayons. Throughout the remainder of the school year and into the next, that "stuff" was one of Jennifer's favorite things to play with, and her bedroom became a classroom. It's uncertain whether Jennifer was able to teach her Cabbage Patch dolls to read, but she certainly tried hard, and she had grades for each of them in her grade book.

Jennifer wasn't just "playing" school. She was pretending to *be* Mrs. Horton. There are many students like Jennifer who go home from our classrooms every day and pretend that they are us. They talk to their dolls and stuffed animals, and to their family members for that matter, the way we talk to them. They treat their toys and the people in their lives the way we treat them. As a teacher models characteristics or skills, his or her students emulate them in an effort to make them their own. That's why positive role modeling is so important for effective prevention.

Effective prevention teachers do more than explain and exhort students to develop characteristics and skills that help them resist using alcohol and other drugs. Effective prevention teachers *exemplify* these characteristics and skills in their lives. For example, when a teacher lectures on the dangerous effects of nicotine and alcohol on the body, he or she *teaches* one thing. But if that same teacher shows up at a school football game wearing a T-shirt that advertises beer and carrying a pack of cigarettes rolled up in the sleeve, his or her students *learn* something totally different.

Whether we like it or not, who we are as prevention teachers speaks much louder than what we say. To be effective, we have to "practice what we preach." We have to "walk our talk." This leads us to the next characteristic of effective prevention teachers, giving clear and congruent messages.

# Gives Clear and Congruent Messages About Alcohol and Other Drugs

To give clear and congruent messages about alcohol and other drugs, we need to look carefully at our own attitudes and values— and at those of our culture—with regard to alcohol and other drugs. According to a study by Collabolletta et al. published in *Psychology in the Schools*, students observe, challenge, and emulate a teacher's personal attitudes about alcohol and other drug use. So, we need to check out our attitudes about alcohol and other drugs. Are they permissive? Overly judgmental? Moralistic?

The following statements, thoughts, or behaviors portray a *permissive* attitude toward alcohol and other drugs:

- Thinking or saying, "Kids almost *have to* experiment with drugs. It's part of growing up."
- Excusing students' use because it's milder than our own.
- "Protecting" the student from disciplinary action by covering up or ignoring his or her alcohol and other drug use. For example, a basketball coach allowing a hung over star player to sleep through practice in order to sober up.

The following statements, thoughts, or behaviors portray a *judgmental* attitude toward alcohol and other drugs:

- Believing that chemically dependent people are "weak-willed."
- Scapegoating students with labels—"doper," "junkies," "burnouts"—that label them as "bad" persons.
- Punishing students for using without trying to secure help for them.

The following statements, thoughts, or behaviors portray a *moralistic* attitude toward alcohol and other drugs:

- Seeing chemical dependence as a moral weakness.
- Equating a person's problems with alcohol and other drugs to his or her being weak-willed or "loose" in other areas of life.

Adult attitudes that are permissive, judgmental, or moralistic aren't helpful to students. Rather, they only lead to *mixed messages*.

Besides looking at our own attitudes about alcohol and other drugs, we also need to examine the attitudes delivered by the media, which are often permissive and suggest that alcohol and other drug use is attractive, acceptable, even necessary. If we pass these attitudes on to our students, we'll not only confuse them, but dilute—if not destroy—our effectiveness as prevention message-givers.

Permissiveness on the part of an adult sometimes results from the adult's own use or abuse of socially "acceptable" drugs such as alcohol and nicotine. Most of us know that smoking crack or injecting heroin is not acceptable for teenagers. However, we may be much more permissive when it comes to young people's use of alcohol and tobacco. We've all heard some adult say, "My friends and I smoked behind the barn all the time (cough, cough) and I turned out just fine" or "I've been drinking since I was fourteen, and I'm not an alcoholic."

Students sense these subtle, cultural messages that link alcohol and other drug use with normal rites of passage. But such messages contain dangerous attitudes. As effective prevention teachers, we must carefully avoid conveying any message that says that the use of alcohol and other drugs is a "normal" part of growing up. Our students may be confused when they hear us say that it's *not* okay to use alcohol and other drugs, that such use is *not* a "normal" part of growing up. Even so, as responsible adults and important role models, we must take a definite stand against the use of alcohol and other drugs by children or adolescents.

Drinking alcohol or using other drugs is against the law for children and teens. Teachers need to remind students about this and remain firm. Remember, giving students the impression that it might be all right for a sixteen-year-old to have a couple of drinks at a party is giving children permission to break the law. That undermines the effectiveness of laws and rules and also undermines our credibility with students. Students may want to test the law or bend the rules, true. At the same time, however, students also want and need their teachers to draw firm, fair boundaries for them, not to say that a little bit of this or that illegal activity is okay.

By drawing and modeling firm and fair boundaries, we're not saying that we're naive enough to think that all young people won't drink alcohol or use other drugs. Rather, we're saying—and modeling—that children need and deserve to hear the clear message that using alcohol and other drugs is risky, dangerous, and unacceptable behavior. That's why effective prevention teachers share their feelings of concern with their students when they overhear students talking about their alcohol and other drug use. For example, a teacher might say, "When I hear you guys bragging about how loaded you get at weekend parties, it really scares me. I'm concerned about what you're doing to yourselves and your future." Likewise, the effective prevention teacher points out that alcohol and other drug use always has consequences—natural and logical.

Natural consequences are those that happen on their own (for example, hangovers, poor grades, trouble at home). Logical consequences are those imposed by authority (for example, suspension or expulsion from school for possession). Not knowing about these consequences prevents students from learning about limits and boundaries. The effective prevention teacher allows students to experience natural consequences and enforces logical consequences. This helps students make better decisions and develop their own sense of personal responsibility.

Just as effective prevention teachers should not send messages of permissiveness, neither should they convey overly judgmental messages. Students interpret these messages as rigid, controlling, militant, and domineering. Remember, many children live with and love adults who use alcohol and other drugs. Students will become defensive and simply tune out anyone who tries to give them the impression that a parent or other significant adult who uses alcohol and other drugs is bad or wrong. And once students have tuned out, they're unable to accept helpful education about prevention from their teachers.

Students also know that alcohol and other drugs can be used appropriately. Although use of illegal drugs is never appropriate, use of prescription drugs is. Tranquilizers and anti-depressants are vital to many who suffer from mental illness. Hyperactivity in children is often successfully controlled through the use of a prescription drug called ritalin. Without morphine, many cancer patients would suffer excruciating pain. And anyone who has ever had an abscessed tooth knows that a prescribed painkilling drug brings welcome relief.

Students also know that alcohol is used moderately and appropriately by many people. Of course, appropriate alcohol use is harder to define. Vernon Johnson, founder and president emeritus of the Johnson Institute, summed up the ambivalence with which alcohol is regarded in our society by saying, "When you mention alcohol, people either get angry or thirsty." Alcohol is used appropriately in religious rituals such as the Jewish Passover Seder, and in the Christian sacrament of Communion. Many of us will toast a bride and groom with champagne, or have a glass of wine with spaghetti without any ill effects or ensuing problems.

As effective prevention teachers, we can model the appropriate use of alcohol, while making it clear that use by children is not acceptable. Making clear statements, setting clear limits, and explaining why we support those limits is effective role modeling and an effective prevention tool to use in the classroom.

17

Historically, chemical dependence has been viewed as a moral weakness or as something that doesn't happen to "decent" people. Attitudes like these often lurk in recesses we're unaware of—at least until they're challenged in a classroom situation. Our values are shaped, in part, by our culture and society. In the case of alcohol and other drug-use messages, society and the media are important manipulators of our attitudes. Again, to be effective prevention teachers, it's a good idea to examine or re-examine our own value systems and to think about how societal attitudes, as well as media messages, may influence us.

Despite the fact that addiction to alcohol or other drugs has been classified as a disease by the World Health Organization, the American Medical Association, the American Psychological Association, and many other organizations, some people continue to view it as a personal failing. This moralistic notion leads to attitudes and behavior that are judgmental, scornful, and punitive.

A teacher who harbors a negative attitude about chemically dependent people may communicate that attitude to students. In some cases, students may themselves be part of a chemically dependent family. If these students hear messages from a teacher that convey moralistic attitudes, they'll often respond by tuning out and discounting anything and everything the teacher may say about alcohol or other drug use.

Those of us who struggle with permissive, restrictive, or moralistic attitudes about alcohol and other drug use or chemical dependence can get more information to reform our attitudes and clarify the messages we give others. Excellent resources are available from Johnson Institute (see Resources, pages 46-48).

For those of us who learn best by personalizing an experience, it is possible to attend open meetings of Alcoholics Anonymous to hear firsthand stories of recovering people. We can also attend Al-Anon meetings, where those who live with or are concerned about someone who is chemically dependent gather to get help for themselves. There, we can talk with people who have lived with chemical dependence in their family.

Information about Alcoholics Anonymous meetings is available by calling your local Alcoholics Anonymous Intergroup Office.

Similarly, information about Al-Anon meeting locations and times is available by calling the Al-Anon Intergroup Office. We owe it to our students and ourselves to get the facts and to examine our attitudes about alcohol and other drugs and chemical dependence.

The happy medium between permissiveness and being judgmental lies in modeling adult attitudes that uphold laws and rules about alcohol and other drug use, while allowing for individual, cultural, and religious differences. A firm understanding that chemical dependence is a disease and not a moral failing will also help us model and present respectful and well-founded prevention concepts. By examining our own attitudes and values, we can locate the inconsistencies in our own thinking, discover how to convey clear, persuasive, and congruent messages to our students, and learn positive ways to become better role models for prevention.

## Credible and Trustworthy

If prevention teaching is to be effective, students need sound information about alcohol and other drugs. To satisfy that need, teachers must have a certain expertise in what *kinds* of drugs (including alcohol) kids use, the *effects* of those drugs, and the *dangers* associated with their use. (See the list of Resources on pages 46-48.) Just as importantly, kids need to receive this information from role models whom they can believe and trust. Why is this so?

Even though accurate *facts* are important for kids to hear, we know two things about information as a preventive tool. First, information about long-term consequences rarely influences kids because they simply do not think of themselves in terms of being older than they are. Second, presenting negative consequences, even in the form of personal stories by other kids or by celebrities, has little effect on curbing use or changing habits.

According to a study by Botvin et al. published by the National Institute on Drug Abuse Research, we can't assume that young people use alcohol and other drugs because they don't know the consequences. This research shows that kids simply don't relate to long-term risk cautions; kids are rooted in the moment, don't

19

envision themselves as aging, and have no sense of their own mortality. In other words, when it comes to kids, abstract knowledge of the negative long-term consequences of chemical use and abuse is of little prevention value. In fact, kids are often more affected by learning about negative short-term consequences. For example, when it comes to preventing smoking, kids are more apt to choose not to use tobacco because of the short-term consequences (bad breath, stained teeth, stinky clothes) than because of long-term ones (heart disease, lung cancer, other respiratory diseases).

Effective prevention teachers are resources for information, and they convey their knowledge in a factual, timely, and relevant manner. In order to be a credible resource, teachers need sound and accurate information about alcohol, marijuana, inhalants, cocaine/crack, hallucinogens, stimulants, barbiturates, tobacco, and steroids. Likewise, they need a basic understanding of the forms in which each of these drugs is used, the effects of each drug, the dangers associated with use, and the symptoms of use.*

Eiseman et al. in the *Journal of Drug Education*, outline the general categories of factual information that an effective prevention teacher should know. This study suggests that teachers be exposed to a variety of topics, including the following: the role of the school in drug education; pharmacology; models of drug abuse; psychological aspects of drug abuse; legal aspects of drug use (federal, state, and local ordinances and school policies); the media and drug use; and knowledge of alcohol, alcoholism, marijuana, tobacco, and smoking. See pages 46-48 of this manual for a list of resources in which you can find this important information.

One note of caution regarding delivery of alcohol and other drug information. Some professionals in the adolescent chemical dependence field warn us that sometimes information is given that actually teaches use or suggests drugs to use and methods of use that students may not otherwise have thought about. For example, inhalant abuse has become a problem particularly for younger children. Inhalants can be almost any chemical that can be inhaled

---

* You can find this information quickly in David Wilmes' excellent booklet, *Facts About Kids' Use of Alcohol and Other Drugs* (Johnson Institute, 1991).

through the nose or mouth. Professionals who work with such kids in treatment programs warn against naming particular products that can be inhaled, or describing in any detail the ways in which such chemicals are inhaled.

So, while teachers benefit from knowing (being credible) about how students may use various kinds of drugs, we need to be careful about how much information we give to students. That is, we must remain trustworthy. Our students need enough information to stay safe, but not so much information that their curiosity is aroused to the point of wanting to try alcohol or other drugs.

Remember, it's unacceptable for students to use illegal drugs other than those prescribed for medical purposes by a physician. Remember, too, that alcohol and tobacco are illegal drugs for any student and that use of any illegal drug is wrong and carries serious consequences. Thus, the best prevention message we can deliver to our students is that alcohol and other drug use is simply not an option. As effective prevention teachers, we want to provide—without preaching or dramatizing—credible information about alcohol and other drugs, accompanied by a strong no-use message, both of which are supported by a firm foundation of trust between ourselves and our students.

Motivation, patience, hospitality, positive role modeling, clear and congruent messages, credibility and trust. These are the characteristics of the effective prevention teacher. Teachers who possess—or who are striving and willing to develop—these characteristics are well on their way to being influential prevention specialists.

**\*skill (skil)—an ability or proficiency that issues from training or practice.**

# Skills of the Effective Prevention Teacher

According to a study by Hochhauser, published by the *Journal of Alcohol and Drug Education*, the prevention teacher's goal should be to help students find and practice behaviors other than drug-taking to help them deal with the pressures of growing up. We can accomplish this goal by teaching students new life skills that lead to healthier behavior. Who we are, how we relate to our students, what we say, the attitudes and roles we convey, our interpersonal teaching techniques, and our credibility and trustworthiness all can combine to deliver a strong message of prevention and healthy living to our students. We can further enhance our effectiveness as prevention teachers by improving our interpersonal skills, our life skills, and our skills in recognizing problems and referring students to appropriate resources for help. We can also seek out help for ourselves or our own family members if alcohol and other drug use is or becomes a problem.

But first, we must understand why young people use or abuse alcohol and other drugs, as well as what changes can effectively alter such behavior. Understanding these things can help us better determine what approach we will use in our classrooms, improve our own skills, and make a more effective and lasting preventive impact on our students.

## Recognizing Why Kids Use

Sometimes the assumptions we make about why kids use alcohol and other drugs are wrong, dead wrong. Incorrect assumptions can lead us to stimulate learning and behavior change opportunities that are ineffective. For example, researchers have demonstrated that kids who perceive drug use as desirable won't be prevented from using drugs if all we do is teach them to say no.

The study by Botvin corrects some myths about why kids use drugs and helps us understand various motivating factors in young people's drug abuse. The first myth this study contradicts is the notion that kids begin using—or learn to abuse—alcohol and other drugs primarily through peer pressure. The study suggests that peer pressure is not always the source of a kid's alcohol or drug use. Instead, use is often a matter of personal choice.

Another myth is that kids start using drugs by drinking alcohol and smoking cigarettes—that alcohol and nicotine are "pathway" drugs to other drug use. The study reports, however, that kids use different pathways to use that may include alcohol and nicotine, but also inhalants, marijuana, and other drugs as well. The pathway to use, in other words, is not always—and not easily—predictable.

The Botvin study also clarifies *why* kids use, suggesting that they start and use for a variety of reasons. Their motivations may include any of the following:

- To cope with problems
- To achieve a goal
- To deal with not doing well in some area of living
- To cope with difficult or uncomfortable social situations
- In response to advertising and media images and suggestions
- In response to the influence of others

Young people who are most susceptible to drug and other alcohol use have low self-esteem, poor self-confidence, and underdeveloped self-control skills.*

According to Botvin we can approach prevention on at least three levels:

- The environmental level
- The social level
- The personal level

Teachers can intercede on an *environmental level* by working to change ideas, feelings, attitudes, and behaviors that unwittingly accept, allow, and/or encourage student alcohol and other drug use

---

* For more information about why kids use alcohol and other drugs, read *Choices & Consequences®: What To Do When a Teenager Uses Alcohol/Drugs* by Dick Schaefer (Johnson Institute, 1987).

to continue or worsen. Teachers can challenge a school climate that reacts to the problem of alcohol and other drug use in simplistic ways. For example, if school staff tend to minimize the problem of alcohol or other drug abuse ("Well, there may be some beer drinking going on around here, but what the heck, kids will be kids. At least they're not using drugs. . . ."), effective prevention teachers will reply, "Alcohol *is* a drug, and drugs *aren't* for kids."

Second, on a *social level*, and by means of their own role modeling, teachers can decrease the social acceptability of alcohol and other drug use. For example, teachers can encourage and help their students to analyze and discuss the media, advertising, or any other vehicle through which alcohol or other drug use either is sanctioned or is made to look attractive.

Third, teachers can approach prevention on a *personal level* by increasing students' skills to handle stress, by helping to reduce the pressures students must deal with, and by increasing students' self-esteem, confidence, and control. Teachers can accomplish these things by teaching or modeling general adaptive behaviors and by helping students acquire a sense of personal competence through assertiveness and social skills training.

How are teachers to do all this? First of all, we must draw on our motivation, our patience, and our bonding with students; rely on our role modeling and our clear and congruent messages; and base our teaching on the credibility and trust we've built between our students and ourselves. Secondly, we must be willing to learn and hone the skills of an effective prevention teacher. These skills fall into three areas:

- Interpersonal Skills
- Life Skills
- Observation and Referral Skills

## Interpersonal Skills

Strong interpersonal skills are the hallmarks of effective prevention teachers. Teachers with these skills are able to establish trust with their students, communicate well, and understand individual differences among students. Students trust these teachers and believe in what they say and do.

## TRUST BUILDING

A good teacher-student relationship begins with building trust. From the first day of school, the effective prevention teacher nurtures trust and builds on it each day as the school year progresses. Honesty is the foundation of trusting relationships. Open, honest communication allows students to rely on what we say and who we are, as much as it allows us to trust our students' actions and statements.

Teacher-student honesty doesn't mean sharing personal information with students or answering inappropriate questions. Teachers must maintain appropriate limits. However, honesty does mean telling students the truth as we perceive it and within the boundaries we deem appropriate. For example, sometimes the truth is that we don't know an answer to a question. Saying we don't know is the honest answer. Or, if we don't want to answer a question, we can be honest and say so, and then move on.

Trust doesn't coexist with inconsistency and fear. This means that we need to be sure that our classroom rules and consequences are consistent, not always changing. We have to be sure that our reactions are consistent, too. For example, if we show amusement at a student's behavior on Tuesday, we can't punish him or her for that same behavior on Thursday. Students need consistency to feel safe and to trust.

Keeping promises and/or enforcing consequences is equally important in maintaining students' trust. When we promise rewards for certain behavior or for achieving particular goals, following through will reinforce our sincerity and our commitment to the value of the appropriate behavior or goal. For example, if we promise a homework-free weekend if students do well on a test or class project, and if students do well, we need to follow through. We need to follow through even if we find ourselves behind and homework would ease our load. In the same way, if we establish a consequence for inappropriate behavior, (for example, a three-day suspension for smoking at school) we must also follow through. Keeping promises and enforcing consequences contribute both to trust and to quality relationships. They let both parties know the game and the rules to play by.

Students test their teachers. We can be sure that if we draw a line on the floor and tell our students not to step over it, at least one student will put a toe over the line just to see if we mean what we say. This is particularly true of students from dysfunctional families who experience inconsistent rules and broken promises. In order to be trusted, we must reiterate limits and rules and impose appropriate consequences. For example, for the third consecutive Monday, Billy, a fifth grader, claimed that he didn't have his homework done and needed an extension. As he did the past two Mondays, Billy claimed that he was "too sick" to finish his work. Billy's teacher calmly restated the school rule regarding failure to hand in homework on time by saying, "Billy, the school rule says that if you come to class with your homework assignment unfinished, you must have a written excuse from a parent. If you don't have that excuse, you must stay after school and finish the assignment in study hall. If you need help, Billy, I'll be here after school this afternoon to help you."

Billy may not have been pleased with the reaction of his teacher. In fact, his teacher may not have been pleased to stay after school to help Billy. Yet, without limits, rules, and consequences, trust between Billy and his teacher would be impossible. With these things, however, students learn that they can trust us as well as the lines we draw; then students stop testing us, and learn to respect what we say.

## AFFIRMING

The effective prevention teacher is aware of how important it is to be respectful and affirming to students. In order to trust us, students need to feel that their teacher accepts them and will be their advocate. Teachers convey their support of students by listening and believing students, by validating and normalizing their feelings, by helping them cope with their problems, and by praising them and correcting them in respectful ways.

For example, a student who lives in a family where a parent is chemically dependent may say, "I hate my mom (or dad)!" The effective prevention teacher will *not* tell the student that he or she doesn't mean what he or she says. Rather, the teacher will affirm the student by:

- Listening to and believing the student: "I can tell that you feel very angry with your mom (or dad)."
- Validating the student's feelings: "It's okay for you to feel angry the way you do."
- Normalizing the student's feelings: "Lots of kids living in your situation feel just the way you do."
- Helping the student to cope with his or her problem: "Many kids in your situation do something to express their angry feelings so they can let them go. Some kids punch a pillow until they don't feel so angry. Maybe you could try that."

## COMMUNICATING

Effective prevention teachers communicate clearly with their students. Effective communication consists of listening well and—as we've seen—giving clear messages. Listening well means that we focus on what the student is saying. We must stop other activities and turn our attention fully to the student. Giving clear messages means we are direct, honest, and specific about our expectations. For example, "By 8:00 a.m. each day, I expect your previous night's homework assignment on my desk. If you haven't completed the assignment, I expect you to come to me at my desk and explain why."

We know that children who are listened to and who hear clear messages from their teachers are able to exhibit the same skills in their own lives. We also know that teachers who are skilled in communication techniques are able to motivate and interact with students more successfully.

Giving clear messages may require us to consider our communication patterns. All of us send unclear messages at times. Statements such as, "I want you to handle your anger better" or "You are so worked up!" or "Stop being so rambunctious!" may be clear to us but not to our students. Messages must be behavior-specific in order to be clear to a student.

Behavior-specific messages tell the student exactly what behavior we want to see. Rather than stating facts, we ask for a specific action. Telling a student, "I want you to sit without speaking" is a much clearer message than "Settle down." Once we gain skill in delivering clear messages, we can, in turn, challenge our students to ask clearly for what they want, thus teaching them a valuable prevention skill.

We can also give clear messages by responding to a student's question as it is stated, rather than guessing or assuming what the student wants to know. If the question and answer are congruent, the speakers are engaged in the same conversation, resulting in clear communication. For example, if a student asks, "Where is my library book?" and the teacher responds, "We aren't going to the library," the question and answer aren't congruent. Two different conversations are going on here. The student wants to know where the book is. The teacher, however, is "guessing" that the student wants to—or is worried about getting to—go to the library. Clear message giving means responding to the question as it is posed: When the student asks, "Where is my library book?" the congruent response would be something like, "Your book is on the shelf by my desk." If your students hear you giving clear messages, they'll find it easier to learn how to give their own.

## RECOGNIZING AND RESPECTING DIFFERENCES

The final interpersonal skill effective prevention teachers demonstrate and/or need is the ability to understand and work with individual differences in students. In many ways, it would be a lot easier if one student was pretty much like another. If classrooms weren't peopled with students who were different and who needed different reading groups, different math groups, individualized instruction, and the like, teaching might be easier and less challenging, but it would also be far less exciting.

Each student is different from every other. Each student learns, processes information, and reacts differently to stress. Likewise, many of us have great cultural diversity in our classrooms. When we deal with students from other cultures whose values and expectations are different from ours, we confront the values of our own culture and evaluate what we assume are normal expectations.

Effective prevention requires teachers to be aware of cultural diversity, in particular, the various ways different cultures traditionally use alcohol (and, in some instances, other drugs as well). For example, some ethnic groups normally consume wine with meals. What, then, do teachers say to a student from such an ethnic group about under-age drinking? Besides alcohol use, rules about dating, decision-making, expressing feelings, and participating in school activities may also vary among cultural groups. Teachers can see to it that individual differences are discussed openly in the classroom and are respected.

Effective prevention requires that teachers avoid dictating parenting practices to our students' families. Instead, an effective prevention teacher will allow for individual differences in students and affirm parents' rights to make rules and to establish what they understand to be appropriate guidelines. At the same time, however, teachers can encourage the school to offer help for parents in learning prevention skills.*

# Life Skills

Life skills are critical elements for both an effective prevention teacher and for any prevention program. Life skills include processing feelings, decision making, behavioral follow-through, communication skills, and refusal skills. While a complete explanation of these skills is beyond the scope of this book, a few words about each will give a sense of what students need in order to develop each skill. Knowing what students need to prevent alcohol and other drug problems tells teachers, in turn, what skills we need to develop in order to teach students effective prevention techniques.

## PROCESSING FEELINGS

Learning to process feelings gives students a way to work through difficult feelings constructively. Processing feelings means:

1.  Knowing how to identify or "name" what we're feeling

2.  Owning our feelings without blaming them on others

3.  Expressing our feelings appropriately—in ways that aren't harmful to ourselves, to another, or to another's property

---

* See David Wilmes' book, *Parenting for Prevention: How to Raise a Child to Say No to Alcohol/Drugs* (Johnson Institute, 1988) and Wilmes' parent curriculum, *Parenting for Prevention: Raising a Child to Say No to Alcohol and Other Drugs* (Johnson Institute, 1991). Both offer excellent help for parents and thoroughly explain the life skills kids will need in order to resist using alcohol and other drugs.

Whenever we, as teachers, process our feelings in healthy ways, we are doing prevention work. When students know what we're feeling and how we're responding to our feelings, our students are learning that behavior affects other people. Such knowledge can be a valuable motivator to get students to change any of their behaviors that might be harmful or inappropriate.

To communicate our own feelings in a way that gives our students the skills to communicate theirs, we must do so without blame or derision. Using I-statements are best: "I feel angry when you hit Lisa" or "I feel scared when you go so high on the climbing tower" or "I feel happy you worked so hard on your report." Messages like these communicate our feelings, and they're honest and respectful to our students.

## DECISION MAKING

Decision making is a life skill that builds on the ability to process feelings. Decision making is a process by which we:

1. Name the problem
2. Identify the feelings we have about the problem
3. Identify what choices we have for taking action
4. Consider the consequences of each choice
5. Consider resources for helping ourselves make a decision
6. Make a decision.

Sharing this process and skill with students is a powerful prevention technique that will help them handle situations that involve making a choice about alcohol or other drug use.

## BEHAVIORAL FOLLOW-THROUGH

Behavioral follow-through is a skill that supports decision making and enables us to set and to reach our goals. The skill of behavioral follow-through means defining a goal we want to reach and then laying out the steps we need to take in order to reach that goal. Since goals usually are reached over time, behavioral follow-through also includes devising ways, such as self encouragement or self-affirmation, to keep striving toward the goal. The final step in behavioral follow-through is identifying a reward system as a way

31

of congratulating ourselves for persevering and, eventually, attaining our goals. In the case of students, this may take the form of sharing their success with their teacher or negotiating with a parent for a night free from usual chores.

The following outlines a typical behavioral follow-through process:

Goal:     *Get better grades.*

Step 1:   What will I do? *Set aside a study time each day.*

Step 2:   How will I do it? *Be sure to bring home all my supplies; make an assignment notebook; keep TV and radio turned off.*

Step 3:   When will I do it? *Every day, for an hour after supper.*

Step 4:   Where will I do it? *In my room or in the quiet corner of the kitchen.*

Step 5:   Who will help me? *I'll ask my teacher for help in school; I'll ask Dad for help at home.*

Step 6:   What sort of self-affirmation will I give myself to keep at it? *"Good grades are worth the work!" "I'll feel so proud when I see a better report card." "I know I can do this."*

Step 7:   What reward will I give myself when I reach my goal? *I'll share my success with my teacher; or I'll ask my dad for a chore-free night; or I'll treat myself to something—maybe a movie.*

From the standpoint of prevention, helping our students become skilled in behavioral follow-through means equipping them to stick by their choices not to use alcohol and other drugs.

## COMMUNICATING

Although this book already dealt with the skill of communication under interpersonal skills, communication is also clearly a life skill and one that deserves further consideration. As seen earlier, communication skills involve listening well and giving clear messages. Communication skills also include knowing:

- How to be assertive without being belligerent
- How to work effectively in groups with peers
- How to express anger in appropriate ways

For example, let's say you have the following as a class rule: "Once I give a homework assignment in class, I will not repeat it. If a student isn't paying attention and doesn't hear it, it's the student's responsibility to get the assignment from another student after class. I will not repeat an assignment simply because a student is not listening." One day, as you're giving a homework assignment in class, you notice that Teresa, one of your students, is whispering to her friend, Peter. A moment later, Teresa raises her hand and asks, "What's today's homework?"

This is a perfect opportunity not only to communicate a clear message, but to demonstrate communication skills that allow you to be assertive without being belligerent and to express your anger in an appropriate way. You could say: "Teresa, all during the time I was giving today's homework assignment, you were whispering to Peter. I feel angry that you did that, especially now that you're asking me to repeat the assignment. You know the class rule, Teresa. You'll have to get the assignment from someone else after class. For now, I would appreciate your attention."

## RESOLVING CONFLICTS

Resolving conflicts is another important prevention skill that can help students avoid problems associated with alcohol and other drug use. Conflict resolution draws on the skills of decision making and behavioral follow-through. For example, suppose one of your students disagrees with your decision to count classroom participation toward the quarter grade. To effectively demonstrate conflict resolution skills, you could take the following steps:

1. Allow the student to have his or her own opinion.

2. Listen carefully to hear and understand the student's feelings and ideas.

3. Avoid making judgments about the student due to his or her opinions or beliefs.

4. Follow the decision-making process outlined above (name the problem— here, the conflict—identify the feelings you have about the problem, identify what choices you have

for taking action, consider the consequences of each choice, consider resources for helping yourself make a decision) and then make a decision based on your best professional judgment and the policies and objectives of the school for which you work.

Being skilled in conflict resolution does not mean giving in or being forced to bend one's principles. Using the example above, as a teacher, you will probably continue to count classroom participation toward a student's quarter grade. At the same time, you will also be teaching the student how to constructively assert himself or herself when someone disagrees with a position he or she holds. You will be showing students that they possess the power to resolve conflicts constructively and to think and act independently.

## ASSERTIVENESS

When it comes to prevention, assertiveness skills translate into *refusal skills*, skills that empower us to say no to high-risk behavior. Refusal skills give students ways of saying no firmly, forcefully, clearly, but gently—ways that won't alienate friends or make students feel like "nerds." In addition to resisting the use of alcohol and other drugs, refusal skills also help students resist pressure to skip school, shoplift, and engage in sexual activity or other high-risk behavior. Effective prevention teachers pass on refusal skills to their students in three ways:

1.  By instilling confidence in students

2.  By allowing students to practice assertive refusal skills in the classroom

3.  By reinforcing individuality

Effective prevention teachers instill confidence in their students when they point out or give feedback on instances of good behavior; for example, "Way to go, Ted! You held your temper when you felt upset over your wrong answer, and you worked hard to correct it and get it right!" Through discussions and/or role plays of problem situations, teachers allow students to practice assertive refusal skills. Finally, teachers can reinforce individuality by complimenting or drawing attention to a student's unique qualities and/or abilities; for example, "Thanks so much for your great sense of humor, Alicia. You help us all laugh at ourselves."

Students who have mastered the important life skills of feeling processing, decision-making, behavioral follow-through, communication, conflict resolution, and assertiveness/refusal skills tend to achieve more in school and more in the workplace as adults. They are also less inclined to use alcohol and other drugs, and that's what prevention is all about.

## TEACHING, MODELING, AND REINFORCING LIFE SKILLS

Ensuring student mastery of life skills involves sound educational techniques. The following simple approach is effective in teaching prevention concepts and behavior: instruct, provide practice, reinstruct, provide more practice. For example, when effective prevention teachers teach students to make decisions, they walk them through the steps of the decision-making process so that they understand each step. Next, they give students opportunities to practice their decision-making skills. Finally, they check students' mastery and provide more practice.

There are other effective ways to teach and reinforce life skills. One way is through modeling. For example, by allowing students to watch us make a real decision that affects them, we can demonstrate effective decision-making skills. Modeling, as we have seen, is more than instruction. It also involves teaching by example and living what we teach.

A second way of teaching life skills is through reinforcement. We reinforce positive skill-building by rewarding students immediately when we observe them using a life skill successfully: "I'm glad to see you made a thoughtful decision about running for student council. Good job!" Words like these encourage students to continue to use life skills as they negotiate their way through their own lives.

Students must also be allowed to make mistakes as they practice life skills. No one does anything perfectly the first time. By allowing for mistakes, we allow students to learn at their own rate and to grow in their skills without fear of failure or recrimination. If exercises that practice the life skills are low-risk, students will see them as just another classroom activity that is part

35

of their overall learning experience and will not fear taking the risk or making mistakes.

Probably the best way to teach life skills is through cooperative learning techniques. Involving students in dyads or small groups allows them to learn, try out, and practice life skills with one another. The smaller group environment allows students to bond and build trust between and among themselves. It also forms the foundation of a support network to which students can turn when in trouble or when faced with difficult decisions—whether about alcohol and other drugs or other important life choices.

## Observation and Referral Skills

In addition to interpersonal skills and life skills, there is one more category of skills that effective teachers of prevention either possess and/or need to develop— observation and referral skills. These are the ability to recognize problems in students and refer them to appropriate resources for help. Most teachers know how to do this in the area of special education or psychological services. The same skills apply in helping students who either have alcohol and other drug problems themselves or who are being harmfully affected by the alcohol and other drug use of someone else.

Because of the in-depth, daily, and long-term contact they have with students, teachers are often the first to detect a student with a problem. That problem may show itself in subtle ways: less motivation or enthusiasm; less interaction in the classroom or with peers; a drop in grades; work not done or work completed with less care; or decreased willingness to contribute in class. Or, the problem may be overt: acting out, absenteeism, falling asleep in class, skipping classes, or quarreling with peers. Whether the problem is subtle or overt, the teacher may be the first to observe a change in attitude or behavior that warrants further investigation.*

---

* To learn more about the changes in students that may signal further problems, see *Choices & Consequences®: What To Do When a Teenager Uses Alcohol/Drugs* by Dick Schaefer (Johnson Institute, 1987). The films/videos *Different Like Me* and *Twee, Fiddle and Huff* (see Resources on pages 46-48 of this booklet) are also good resources.

Effective prevention teachers who have built strong student relationships are strategically placed to encourage a student to discuss a problem. Once the problem is identified, an effective prevention teacher will rely on his or her previous knowledge of helpful resources to refer a student. If a student is obviously using alcohol or other drugs in school, teachers check the school policy and then make an appropriate referral to get help for the student. Depending on the school policy, that referral may be to the School Assistance Program (SAP), to the school chemical health specialist, or to an outside mental or chemical health professional who is knowledgeable about chemical use, assessment, identification, and treatment.

According to the study by Collabolletta et al., teachers who act as part of a larger, multidisciplinary team (for example, as part of a school-wide SAP) are most effective in recognizing and referring students with alcohol or other drug problems. Being part of a team lets teachers talk with school or community mental health specialists to determine the best way to approach such students. By eliciting help from all quarters—from parents, school counselors, school chemical health professionals, and outside community resources—teachers can help their students in the most effective way.

We teachers have to accept that we may not always be able to spot a student who is using alcohol and other drugs until that use causes problems in school. However, we must be careful not to casually write off problems associated with use as being the result of a family crisis or possibly as a bad attitude on the part of the student. Instead, the effective prevention teacher views changes in performance, attendance, participation, or activity level as possible symptoms of alcohol and other drug use. Mood swings, irritability, and personality changes also may be indicative of use. Any of these symptoms may suggest an underlying cause warranting further investigation and, perhaps, a referral for help.

Students who are part of a family in which one or more members are actively chemically dependent may exhibit problems not necessarily associated with the student's own use as much as with the dysfunction resulting from a family member's chemical abuse. We know that chemical dependence is a disease. We know, too, that those students who live with someone who is chemically dependent can develop self-defeating ways of coping with the disease. These self-defeating ways of coping with another's problem, sometimes referred to as co-dependence, progress in severity as the chemically dependent family member gets worse.

Co-dependence usually affects a student's attitudes, behavior, and school performance. Some students may try to over-achieve or be the perfect student. Others may rebel and act out, become the class clown, or withdraw in silence. Whatever the behavior, effective prevention teachers should recognize it as a problem and refer such students to get help through counseling, through education, or from a support group.

Of importance to prevention teachers is how the effects of problems like alcohol and other drug use or co-dependence are expressed within the school setting. Teachers need to know:

- What happens to school attendance and performance as students become harmfully involved with alcohol and other drugs?

- How does living in a chemically dependent family affect behavior and attitudes in the classroom?

- What physical symptoms would a student who is using alcohol, inhalants, or tobacco have?

Knowing the answers to these questions will clarify the appropriate steps to take in referring a student for help.

To make a difference as effective prevention teachers, we don't need to become diagnosticians, interventionists, or therapists. However, we do need to be able to keep our eyes and ears open, to pay attention to changes in our students' behavior, and to make appropriate, helpful referrals. Effective prevention teachers understand these roles and work to develop their observation and referral skills.

If developing and exercising the skills of an effective prevention teacher seem a bit daunting, don't panic. And don't give up! Just as your students can learn these skills, so can you. Resources and training in life skills development are available. For example, the Johnson Institute offers numerous training opportunities for prevention teachers and can even design training that's geared to your specific needs. With the help of such training, you, too, can become an effective prevention teacher.

# Resolving Personal Issues

Effective prevention teachers realize that they're not exempt from the problems that plague the rest of the population. Teachers get divorced, lose a spouse to death, have mental health concerns, and experience financial, legal, parenting, and physical crises like everyone else. And, based on the fact that over 28 million Americans, men and women alike, have had their lives deeply affected by a parent's chemical dependence,* we can assume that many teachers come from families that were harmfully affected by chemical dependence.

For those of us who work with young people, it's particularly important to resolve such problems outside the workplace. If we bring our problems, such as co-dependent or dysfunctional behavior due to parental or spousal chemical dependence, into our classrooms, we risk affecting our interactions with our students and our teaching of healthy living skills. We have a responsibility to ourselves and to our students to get help and support for our own problems *outside* the classroom.

Admitting our problem and the pain it causes can lead us to seek and find help. Sometimes, teaching children about the problems that often result from alcohol or other drug use brings our own buried pain to the surface. We may be tempted to avoid prevention topics in order to avoid such pain, but doing so may be a disservice not only to our students, but also to ourselves.**

Fortunately, many resources are available. Almost every one of us lives or works within driving distance of an Al-Anon or Alcoholics Anonymous meeting. Most communities provide some sort of counseling and/or mental health services. Many schools offer quality counseling and referral services through an employee assistance program. Seeking help for our own problems will enhance our ability to be effective prevention teachers.

---

* M. Hindman, "Children of Alcoholic Parents," *Alcohol, Health and Research World*, National Institute on Alcoholism and Alcohol Abuse, 1975-6:2-6.

** See Timmen L. Cermak, M.D. *Diagnosing and Treating Co-dependence: A Guide for Professionals Who Work with Chemical Dependents, Their Spouses, and Children* (Johnson Institute, 1986).

# Self-Test

Now that you've read about the characteristics and skills of effective prevention teachers, you might want to evaluate yourself. The following set of statements is designed to give you an opportunity to assess your own characteristics, skills, and knowledge—and to check your own beliefs and attitudes—about effective prevention concepts.

Designate whether you agree or disagree with each statement by circling True or False. Afterward, turn to page 42 to find the correct answers. Your responses will suggest areas you may wish to improve in order to become a more effective prevention teacher—a teacher who can make a difference.

1. Alcohol and other drug prevention should begin in junior high.

   True    False

2. Conveying accurate, factual information about the dangers of alcohol and other drug use is the most effective means of preventing the problem of chemical abuse or chemical dependence.

   True    False

3. Effective prevention teachers must be skilled in diagnosis, intervention, and therapy.

   True    False

4. Peer pressure is not the primary motivator or reason kids start using alcohol and other drugs.

   True    False

5. Young people always use tobacco and alcohol as pathways to other drugs.

   True    False

6. Kids with low self-esteem experience more problems with alcohol and other drug use.

   True    False

7. Nurturing strong relationships with students is an effective prevention approach.

   True    False

8. Setting limits on behavior for young people should be left to parents in the home.

   True    False

9. When a teacher tells a student, "I want you to handle your anger better," he or she is conveying a clear message.

   True    False

10. Teachers can be primary life skill educators, helping students learn how to live as well as how to think.

    True    False

11. Teachers should not view changes in participation, enthusiasm, grades, or level of class preparation as indicative of serious student problems.

    True    False

12. Students coping with a family member's chemical dependence may exhibit behavior similar to a student who has a personal alcohol or other drug problem.

    True    False

# Self-Test Answers

1. Alcohol and other drug prevention should begin in junior high.

False. Prevention should begin as early as possible and continue building upon learned skills each year, at least through grade twelve, and even into college and beyond.

2. Conveying accurate, factual information about the dangers of alcohol and other drug use is the most effective means of preventing the problem of chemical abuse or chemical dependence.

False. Research has shown that information alone is not effective in preventing use and abuse of alcohol and other drugs among young people.

3. Effective prevention teachers must be skilled in diagnosis, intervention, and therapy.

False. The role of the effective prevention teacher is to identify problems and make referrals based on observable classroom behavior. Only professionals skilled in diagnosis, intervention, and therapy or treatment of adolescent alcohol or other drug problems should perform such functions.

4. Peer pressure is not the primary motivator or reason kids start using alcohol and other drugs.

True. Kids use alcohol and other drugs for a variety of reasons. Motivations can include using to cope with problems; to ease social discomfort; in response to not doing well in another area; in response to media messages, etc.

5. Young people always use tobacco and alcohol as pathways to other drugs.

False. A number of different drugs can be pathways to a young person's drug use. Marijuana and inhalants, along with alcohol and tobacco (nicotine), are often the "pathway" or "gateway" drugs used by young people.

6. Kids with low self-esteem experience more problems with alcohol and other drug use.

True. Low self-esteem and lack of self-confidence, as well as difficulty with self-control, are factors that make kids more susceptible to alcohol and other drug use problems.

7. Nurturing strong relationships with students is an effective prevention approach.

True. Current research is showing us that interpersonal relationships between student and teacher are more important than conveying factual information or consequences of alcohol and other drug use.

8. Setting limits on behavior for young people should be left to parents in the home.

False. Effective prevention teachers can and should set clear limits, expectations, and consequences for behavior in the classroom. Further, teachers play a powerful role in conveying norms: teachers can be singularly effective in conveying ideas such as alcohol and other drug use by students is unacceptable in any circumstance.

9. When a teacher tells a student, "I want you to handle your anger better," he or she is conveying a clear message.

False. Clear messages must be behavior-specific, i.e., telling a student what behavior we want to see. Rather than stating facts, we ask for a specific action.

10. Teachers can be primary life skill educators, helping students learn how to live as well as how to think.

True. An effective prevention teacher educates students in the areas of processing feelings, making decisions, behavioral follow-through, communication, conflict resolution, and refusal skills.

11. Teachers should not view changes in participation, enthusiasm, grades, or level of class preparation as indicative of serious student problems.

False. Such subtle changes in student behavior may, indeed, indicate a personal or family problem with alcohol or other drug use and should be investigated early, before more serious problems, such as acting out behavior, develop.

12. Students coping with a family member's chemical dependence may exhibit behavior similar to a student who has a personal alcohol or other drug problem.

True. Such students often exhibit withdrawing or acting out behavior similar to that shown by students with personal alcohol or other drug use problems. These students need counseling or other help to develop healthy coping techniques and resolve difficulties in dealing with problems at home.

# Setting Goals

Based on what you discovered in the preceding self-test, you may wish to set goals to achieve greater expertise as an effective prevention teacher. Your goals may include taking courses in prevention and alcohol and other drug education. Seminars or short-courses in life skills techniques may help you learn more about topics such as teaching refusal and decision-making skills, building self-esteem among students, assertiveness training, or conflict resolution.

Making appropriate and effective referrals may also require you to set specific goals to learn what school and community resources are available. What resources are available right in your own school? Is there a chemical health specialist on staff? Can the school counselor help with student problems related to alcohol and other drug use? Are self-help groups available within the school?

Investigating community resources may include locating quality resources with expertise in identification, assessment, intervention, and treatment of young people's alcohol and other drug problems. Knowledge of good referral sources for parents and families is also helpful.

The goals you set will help you gain competence in developing the characteristics, skills, and referral resources you need to really make a difference in the lives of your students.

# Bibliography

Aubrey, R.F. "Drug Education: Can Teachers Really Do the Job?" *Teachers College Record* 72:3 (1971): 417-422.

Botvin, Gilbert J. "Prevention of Adolescent Substance Abuse Through the Development of Personal and Social Competence". *Preventing Adolescent Drug Abuse: Intervention Strategies* Monograph No. 47. Rockville, MD: National Institute on Drug Abuse Research, 1983.

Christensen, Linda. *Facts, Feelings, Family, and Friends: Alcohol and Other Drug-Use Prevention Through Life Skills Development (Curriculum for Grades K-6).* Minneapolis: Johnson Institute, 1990.

Collabolletta, E.A., A.J. Fossbender, and T.E. Bratter. "The Role of the Teacher with Substance-Abusing Adolescents in Secondary Schools." *Psychology in the Schools* 20 (1983): 450-455.

Eiseman, Seymour, James Robinson III, Vicente Zapata. "M.D.A.: A Multi-Disciplinary Approach for Teacher Effectiveness Training in Drug Education." *Journal of Drug Education* 14:4 (1984).

Freeman, Shelley MacKay. *From Peer Pressure to Peer Support: Alcohol/Drug Prevention Through Group Process.* Minneapolis: Johnson Institute, 1989.

Goodstat, M.S. "School-Based Drug Education in North America: What Is Wrong? What Can Be Done?" *Journal of School Health* 56:7 (1986).

Hoch, Loren L., Janice Olszowy. "What Do Teachers Say?: Another Look at Drug Education." *Journal of Alcohol and Drug Education* 26:3 (1981).

Hochhauser, M. "Drug Education: Who Teaches What to Whom?" *Journal of Alcohol and Drug Education* 25:2 (1980): 61-67.

Jones, Randall M., Kathleen Kline, Sue A. Habkirk, and Amos Sales. "Teacher Characteristics and Competencies Related to Substance Abuse Prevention," *Journal of Drug Education* 20:3 (1990).

Wilmes, David J. *Parenting for Prevention: How to Raise a Child to Say No to Alcohol/Drugs.* Minneapolis: Johnson Institute, 1988.

# Resources

The following curricula, books, workbooks, booklets, films and videocassettes are available from Johnson Institute. To order any of these resources, call or write:

Johnson Institute
7205 Ohms Lane
Minneapolis, MN 55439-2159

United States and Canada:
800-231-5165 or
612-831-1630

## Curricula

Christensen, Linda. *Facts, Feelings, Family, and Friends: Alcohol and Other Drug Use Prevention Through Life Skills Development* (A Curriculum for Grades K-6).

Freeman, Shelley MacKay. *From Peer Pressure to Peer Support: Alcohol/Drug Prevention Through Group Process* (A Curriculum for Grades 7-12).

Schmidt, Teresa, and Thelma Spencer. *Building Trust, Making Friends: Four Group Activity Manuals for High-Risk Students.*

*Della the Dinosaur Talks About Violence and Anger Management* (Grades K-6).

*Peter the Puppy Talks About Chemical Dependence in the Family* (Grades K-6).

*Tanya Talks About Chemical Dependence in the Family* (Grades 6-8).

*Thomas Barker Talks About Divorce and Separation* (Grades K-6).

Wilmes, David J. *Parenting for Prevention—A Parent Education Curriculum: Raising a Child to Say No to Alcohol and Other Drugs.*

# Books

Anderson, Gary L. *When Chemicals Come to School: The Student Assistance Program Model.*

Cermak, Timmen L., M.D. *Diagnosing and Treating Co-dependence: A Guide for Professionals Who Work with Chemical Dependents, Their Spouses and Children.*

Cohen, Peter R., M.D. *Helping Your Chemically Dependent Teenager Recover: A Guide for Parents and Other Concerned Adults.*

Fleming, Martin. *Conducting Support Groups For Students Affected by Chemical Dependence: A Guide for Educators and Other Professionals.*

Johnson, Vernon E. *Intervention: How to Help Someone Who Doesn't Want Help—A Step-by-Step Guide for Families and Friends of Chemically Dependent Persons.*

Leite, Evelyn, and Pamela Espeland. *Different Like Me: A Book for Teens Who Worry About Their Parents' Use of Alcohol/Drugs.*

Moe, Jerry, and Peter Ways, M.D. *Conducting Support Groups for Elementary Children K-6: A Guide for Educators and Other Professionals.*

Schaefer, Dick. *Choices & Consequences®: What to Do When a Teenager Uses Alcohol/Drugs—A Step-by Step System that Really Works.*

Wilmes, David, J *Parenting for Prevention: How to Raise a Child to Say No to Alcohol/Drugs.*

# Workbooks

Fleming, Martin. *How to Stay Clean and Sober: A Relapse Prevention Guide for Teenagers.*

Sassatelli, Jean. *Breaking Away: Saying Goodbye to Alcohol/Drugs—A Guide to Help Teenagers Stop Using Chemicals.*

Zarek, David, and James Sipe. *Can I Handle Alcohol/Drugs?: A Self-Assessment Guide for Youth.*

*A Story About Feelings* (Coloring Book).

*Twee, Fiddle and Huff* (Coloring Book).

47

# Booklets

Alcoholism: A Treatable Disease.

Anderson, Gary L. Enabling in the School Setting.

Anderson, Gary L. Solving Alcohol/Drug Problems in Your School.

Chemical Dependence and Recovery: A Family Affair.

Chemical Dependence: Yes, You Can Do Something.

Cloninger, C. Robert, M.D. Genetic and Environmental Factors Leading to Alcoholism.

Daley, Dennis C., and Judy Miller. Recovery & Relapse Prevention for Parents of Chemically Dependent Children.

Daley, Dennis C., and Judy Miller. When Your Child Is Chemically Dependent.

The Family Enablers.

Leite, Evelyn. How It Feels to Be Chemically Dependent.

Leite, Evelyn. Detachment: The Art of Letting Go While Living with an Alcoholic.

Recovery of Chemically Dependent Families.

Why Haven't I Been Able to Help?

Wilmes, David, J. Facts About Kids' Use of Alcohol and Other Drugs.

# Films/Videocassettes

Another Chance to Change: A Teenager's Struggle with Relapse and Recovery. Color, 30 minutes.

Back to Reality. Color, 31 minutes.

Choices & Consequences®: Intervention with Youth in Trouble with Alcohol/Drugs. Color 33 minutes.

Different Like Me®: For Teenage Children of Alcoholics. Color, 31 minutes.

Enabling: Masking Reality. Color, 22 minutes.

Intervention: Facing Reality. Color, 30 minutes.

A Story About Feelings. Animated, Color, 16 minutes.

Twee, Fiddle and Huff. Animated, Color, 16 minutes.

Where's Shelley? Color, 14 minutes.